DATE DUE

796.352
WIL
C.1

Will, Sandra
Golf for fun!

$17.95
BC#34880000108329

DATE DUE	BORROWER'S NAME 21
7/16/02	Jose Horta
11/27/07	Fernando Vega
06	Stacey
08	Jocon Brook 217

796.352   BC#34880000108329 $17.95
WIL
C.1

Will, Sandra
Golf for fun!

GOLF
FOR FUN!

By Sandra Will

Content Adviser: Tom Sutter, PGA Class A Golf Professional, New York, New York
Reading Adviser: Frances J. Bonacci, Reading Specialist, Cambridge, Massachusetts

C O M P A S S   P O I N T   B O O K S

M I N N E A P O L I S ,   M I N N E S O T A

Compass Point Books
3109 West 50th Street, #115
Minneapolis, MN 55410

Visit Compass Point Books on the Internet at *www.compasspointbooks.com*
or e-mail your request to *custserv@compasspointbooks.com*

Photographs ©: Getty Royalty Free, front cover (left), front cover (background), 5 (left), 5 (right), 9, 12 (bottom left), 13 (center), 13 (bottom), 21, 42 (bottom), 42(right), 43 (top right), 43 (left), 45 (center), 47; Photos.com, front cover (right), back cover, 23; David Cannon/Getty Images, 4, 12 (right); Sean Garnsworthy/Getty Images, 7; Courtesy of Bryan Jaffe, 10-11; Christie K. Silver, 13 (top left); Harry How/Getty Images, 15, 16-17, 34-35; Mark Dadswell/Getty Images, 19; Corel, 25, 45 (top right); Stuart Franklin/Getty Images, 27, 31; Warren Little/Getty Images, 29; Getty Images, 33, 40; Andrew Redington/Getty Images, 36-37; Jeff Gross/Getty Images, 38-39; Anton Want/Getty Images, 41; Arttoday 42 (bottom left), 44 (center), 45 (bottom left); Comstock, 43 (bottom right); Hulton Archive/Getty Images, 43 (center); Paul Severn/Getty Images, 43 (center right); Gary Newkirk/Getty Images, 44.

Editor: Elizabeth Bond/Bill SMITH STUDIO
Photo Researchers: Sandra Will, Sean Livingstone, and Christie Silver/Bill SMITH STUDIO
Designer: Colleen Sweet/Bill SMITH STUDIO

Library of Congress Cataloging-in-Publication Data
Will, Sandra.
Golf for fun! / by Sandra Will.
p. cm. – (Sports for fun!)
Summary: Describes the sport of golf and presents information on the basic equipment, golf courses, scoring, technique, rules of play and golf etiquette.
Includes bibliographical references and index.
ISBN 0-7565-0486-4 (hardcover : alk. paper)
1. Golf–Juvenile literature. [1. Golf.] I. Title. II. Series.
GV968.W55 2003
796.352–dc21

2003006672

Table of Contents

Ground Rules

Playing the Game

People, Places, and Fun

Note: In this book, there are two kinds of vocabulary words. Golf Words to Know are words specific to golf. They are in **bold** and are defined on page 46. Other Words to Know are helpful words that aren't related only to golf. They are in ***bold and italicized.*** These are defined on page 47.

Everybody Golf!

Have you ever played golf? Every year, people of all ages grab their clubs and flock to golf courses around the world. The sport of golf has a long, rich history that dates back to the 14th century. No one knows for sure who invented the game of golf or when it was first played. Many people believe that golf evolved from a game called "chole" that was played in England during the 1300s. In 1421, golf made its way to Scotland, which is considered to be the home of modern golf. Over the past six centuries, golf has grown into one of the most popular sports in the world.

Goal of the Game

Golf can be played as either an individual or a team sport. Each player tries to hit the ball into every hole on the course. For each hole, golfers try to use the least number of **strokes** (see p.10). At the end of the **round,** or game, the winner is the player with the lowest score, or fewest strokes.

*Golf balls only weigh 1.6 ounces (46 grams), but they have an interesting design. All golf balls are shaped like **spheres**. Tiny dimples cover the entire surface of the ball. The dimples allow the ball to travel longer distances than balls without dimples.*

The Big Green

The game of golf is played on a course. The golf course is the entire land area where play is allowed. Most golf courses have 18 holes, but some only have nine. The average length of a golf course is 5,500 to 7,000 yards (5,029 to 6,401 meters). Each hole begins at the **teeing area.** The **fairway** connects the teeing area and the green. The green is the level area that contains the hole. A flagstick marks the location of the hole, which helps players aim more *accurately* from a long way away. Look at the picture to learn the names of the parts of the golf course.

Different types of grass cover each section of the course. The grass affects the speed and direction of the ball, adding another challenge to the game. On the fairway, the grass is medium length, and the height of the grass keeps the ball from rolling long distances.

teeing area

fairway

bunker

rough

green

hole

The green has very short grass, which causes the ball to roll and move faster. In the **rough,** the grass is 2–3 inches (5–8 centimeters) tall. The grass gets between a player's club and the ball, making it difficult to hit a good shot.

Did You Know?
A golf course that borders the ocean is called a **links course.**

7

One, Two, Three, Four

The game of golf is *unique.* In other sports, the team or individual with the highest score wins, but in golf, the lowest score wins!

Golfers can either play by themselves or compete against other players. When two people play against each other, it is called a **pairing.** During some competitions, golfers play in pairs. People also play golf in groups of three or four: a threesome or foursome. A foursome is the most common grouping in golf. Four players travel the course together and play each hole.

In team golf, groups of players compete on the same team and add their scores together. Two players usually play on each team. Players from each team alternate, or take turns, at each hole. Like individuals, the team with the lowest score wins.

Players must take their turn at each hole without causing a delay in the game.

Tournament Play

Golf competitions take place at tournaments. A tournament usually has more than one round of golf and often lasts several days. Players or teams compete in each round trying to use the fewest number of strokes. The scores in each round are added together, and the player, or team, with the lowest total score at the end of the tournament is crowned the winner.

Par for the Course

How do you keep score in golf? Players count the number of strokes they make during each round. Every time you swing your club at the ball, it counts as a stroke–even if you miss the ball entirely. When you swing at the ball and miss, it is called an airball, or whiff.

Golfers try to make **par** on each hole. Par is the number of strokes an expert golfer would use to finish playing a hole. Golf courses have par-three, par-four, and par-five holes. The number tells the *maximum* number of strokes a player may use to make par. Golfers keep track of their scores for each round on a scorecard.

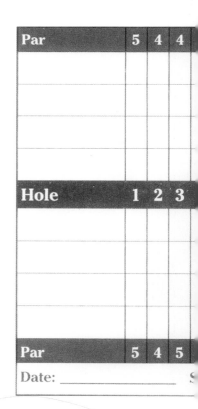

Par		5	4	4
Hole		1	2	3
Par		5	4	5
Date: _____				S

Golfers are responsible for the correctness of the score recorded for each hole on their cards.

Fly Like an Eagle

Golfers have special names to describe their performance on each hole. Most of the names are based on how many strokes under or over par you score on a hole. Here are the most common scoring terms used in golf:

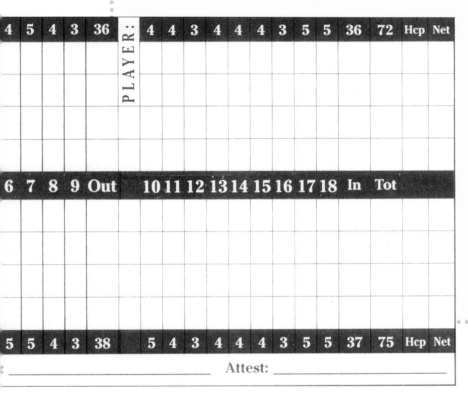

Term	Description
Ace	A hole in one stroke
Eagle	Two strokes under par
Birdie	One stroke under par
Bogey	One stroke over par
Double bogey	Two strokes over par

Suit Up

In golf, each player decides what he or she will wear on the course. Most golfers wear slacks or shorts with a special polo shirt, known as a golf shirt. Some players wear a sweater vest. All golf clothing has one thing in common: It is comfortable and allows the player to move easily. Unlike most other sports, golfers don't have to wear special protective equipment or uniforms— most golf clothing would look OK if worn off the golf course. Players do, however, use special types of equipment to help them play the game.

Clubs come in a variety of shapes and sizes. Most clubs are made out of metal or wood.

Players wear gloves to prevent blisters from forming on their fingers and hands. Gloves also keep the club from slipping when a player has sweaty hands.

A tee raises the ball off the ground at the teeing area, allowing a golfer to hit the ball better. Tees are made of wood, are about 2 inches (5 cm) long, and can only be used in the teeing area.

Golfers wear special shoes with cleats, or spikes, on the bottom. Cleats keep a golfer from slipping on the grass during a swing.

Players use bags to hold their clubs as they move along the golf course.

Which One?

Golfers are allowed to carry up to a maximum of 14 clubs in their bags. A standard set of clubs includes eight **irons,** four **woods,** and a **putter.** Players also use a special club called a **wedge.** Each club has a different amount of loft. The loft is the tilt on the club's face that helps get the ball into the air. The more loft the club has, the higher the ball will go in the air. The ball will also travel a shorter distance when it lands. Clubs with less loft help golfers hit the ball longer distances.

A golfer needs to think about the differences in clubs before choosing the right one. You should select the club that will allow you to make the most accurate shot. The more accurately you hit the ball, the fewer strokes you will need to finish each hole.

The Caddie

Professional golfers use a person called a **caddie** to carry their clubs. Caddies know information about each golf course, such as the distances on every hole. They often discuss strategies with players and help them make their club selections. Caddies also help players keep track of their scores on their scorecards.

Justin Leonard (right) discusses his club selection with his caddie during the 2000 PGA Championship.

Teeing Off

During a round of golf, every hole begins with a tee shot. A golfer stands in the teeing area and places his or her ball on a tee. Then the player prepares to swing and hit the ball as far as possible. Each golfer tries to move the ball from the teeing area to the green with a single tee shot. To make a good tee shot, a player must keep the ball "in play." Any ball that does not go **out-of-bounds** is in play. When the ball travels out-of-bounds, the golfer must use extra strokes to reach the hole.

Tee shots are called **drives** on par-four or par-five holes. On these longer holes, golfers must drive the ball farther to reach the hole. Most players cannot reach the green with a single stroke on these holes and must make a second drive from the fairway without using a tee.

Did You Know?

Each round of golf begins at a particular tee time. A tee time is the appointment a golfer makes in advance to play a round of golf. Golfers schedule tee times so that too many people do not show up to play at the same time.

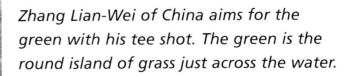

Zhang Lian-Wei of China aims for the green with his tee shot. The green is the round island of grass just across the water.

The Approach

Once a player drives the ball from the tee to the fairway, he or she is ready to make an approach shot. The approach is a shot to the green that is made anywhere on the course—except the tee. Before they make their approach shot, golfers examine the ball's **lie.** The lie is the spot where the golf ball comes to rest on or near the course.

After deciding the best shot to make, the player selects a club and aims for the green. Usually, golfers use one approach shot to move the ball from the fairway to the green, but sometimes they must make a second approach shot to the hole.

Nick Faldo of England hits his approach shot from the fairway and tries to move his ball to the green.

Did You Know?

A **divot** is a hole in the course that golfers make with their clubs or shoes.

Hole Out

What happens when the approach shot does not land on the green? Golfers use special types of short shots (see p. 24) to move the ball onto the green. After the ball is on the green, the player is ready to **putt** the ball into the hole. Before they putt, golfers look at the slope of the green.

Putting a ball into a hole would be easy if greens were made completely flat. But most greens have little hills and dips built into the ground, making a putted ball break, or move, in different directions. Before putting, a golfer plans a careful path for the ball to travel. Watch out! A bad putt might make a ball break the wrong way; it could roll in the opposite direction of the hole and keep on rolling!

Golfers try to sink the ball into the hole with one putt, but if they don't, they must keep putting until they finish the hole, or **"hole out."** Then, they move to the tee of the next hole and prepare to tee off again. Golfers play each hole in the same order until they finish their round.

Swing Away!

What is the best way to move the ball along the course? A good swing. When a golfer swings the club well, he or she can move the ball to the hole with fewer strokes. Watch out! A bad swing can result in disaster. If a player swings poorly, the ball usually heads just about anywhere—except toward the hole. Golfers make many kinds of swinging errors with different results.

Error	Description
Slice	A severe left-to-right curving shot is called a slice.
Hook	A hook is the opposite of a slice. Hook shots spin from right to left and curve largely to the left.
Push	When a player hits a shot on a straight path to the right of the target, it is called a push.
Pull	A pull is the opposite of a push. The player hits the ball in a straight path to the left of the target.
Fat	When a player hits more of the ground and less of the ball, the ball pops up in the air and falls to the ground quickly. This is known as a fat.

Pitching In

To score well in golf, players must be able to hit accurate, short shots to the hole. Chipping, pitching, and putting are the three basic parts of the **short game.** Players use each of these shots to move the ball to the green from short distances and sink the ball into the hole.

Here is some important information about the parts of the short game:

Pitching: Golfers use pitch shots 30 to 80 yards (37 to 73 m) away from the green. Pitches are generally longer than chip shots and shorter than full shots. Pitch shots stay mostly in the air. The ball travels high into the air and does not roll far when it lands.

Chipping: Players use the chip shot within 30 yards (27 m) of the green. A chip is a very short shot that starts out with an **arc** through the air and bounces on the green. After the ball lands, the short grass of the green allows the ball to roll.

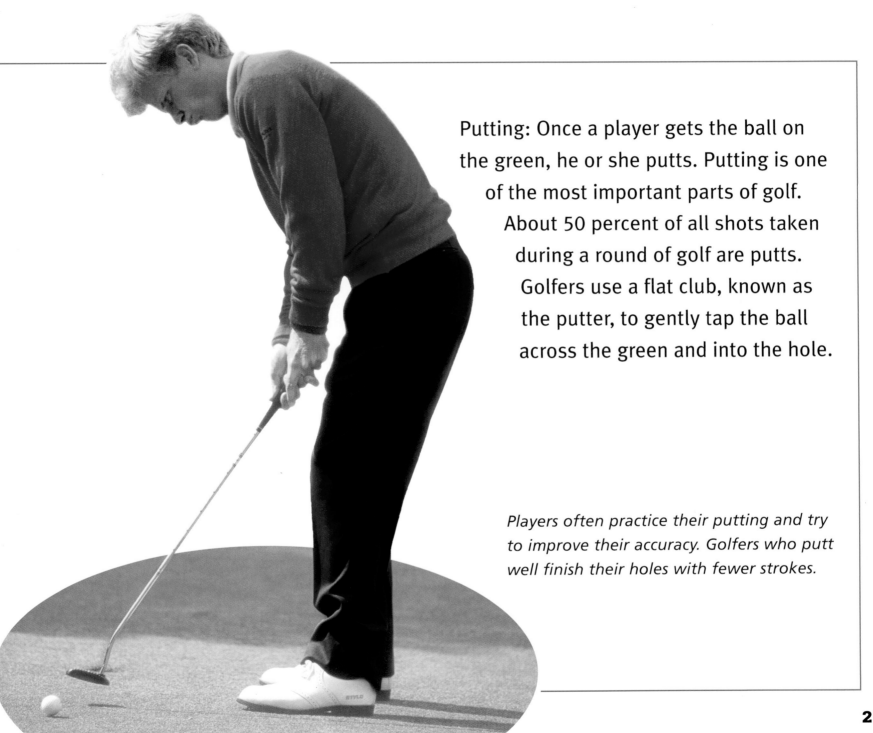

Putting: Once a player gets the ball on the green, he or she putts. Putting is one of the most important parts of golf. About 50 percent of all shots taken during a round of golf are putts. Golfers use a flat club, known as the putter, to gently tap the ball across the green and into the hole.

Players often practice their putting and try to improve their accuracy. Golfers who putt well finish their holes with fewer strokes.

Play It As It Lies

In the game of golf, players cannot move the ball from the position that it lands on the course. They must play the ball as it lies. The ball's lie can cause problems in a golfer's game. Sometimes players hit the ball into a difficult location on the course, which is called "a bad lie." Players are unable to hit the ball cleanly from a bad lie, because something blocks or affects the path of the ball. For example, the ball might land in the rough, on a leaf or a stick, next to a tree, or in a **hazard** (see p. 28).

Players must often use extra strokes to get the ball out of a bad lie. They must first hit the ball into a better playing position. Then they can make a clear shot for the hole. Getting out of difficult situations is part of what makes golf so challenging and exciting!

Padraig Harrington of Ireland struggles with a really bad lie. His ball landed under a tree, and he cannot even stand up straight to shoot!

The Impossible

Sometimes the ball's lie is so impossible that the ball is not playable. This is known as an **unplayable lie.** When the ball is unplayable, golfers must move the ball to a playable position. The distance a player can move the ball depends on where the ball lands. Players are penalized one stroke for an unplayable lie.

At Your Own Risk

Every hole has a series of hazards between the tee and the green. A hazard is an *obstacle* that makes it harder to hole out without using extra strokes. There are two types of hazards: sand and water. Bunkers are a type of hazard filled with sand and are placed just about anywhere on a course—alongside fairways or right next to greens. When a ball lands in the bunker, a player hits as many strokes as it takes to get the ball back onto the grass. Players cannot touch the ground with the club before they hit the ball when they are in the bunker.

A water hazard is any open water, such as an ocean, lake, pond, river, or stream, located on the golf course. When the ball lands in the water, the player is penalized one stroke. He or she has the choice of playing another ball from the spot of the last shot or dropping a ball behind the water hazard. From behind the hazard, the player must hit the ball over the water to reach the hole.

David Dixon of England tries to move his ball from the bunker onto the green without taking extra strokes.

Follow the Rules

Golf is a game of many rules. It would be difficult to learn all of the rules at once, but it is important to learn as many as possible. Here are some of the rules:

• A golfer must play the same ball from the teeing ground into the hole. A player can only change balls in certain cases where the rules allow, such as losing a ball in a water hazard.

• A player must hole out on each hole. Otherwise, he or she will not have a score and will be *disqualified.*

• Players may only get advice from their teammate or caddies. Golfers cannot give playing tips to other players during a game.

• Players must be able to identify their own ball. All players are responsible for playing their own ball.

- If a player loses his or her ball anywhere besides a hazard, he or she can return to where the previous shot was hit and hit another. The player earns a one-stroke penalty.

- A player must locate a lost ball in five minutes. Otherwise, he or she must return to where the ball was played and hit another.

Adam Scott of Australia tries to play his ball from a water hazard while following the rules.

Do's and Don'ts

Golf has a code of conduct, known as etiquette. Etiquette is the sense of manners, politeness, and honesty with which golfers play. All golfers are supposed to be **courteous** and observe the rules of etiquette when they play.

Here are some of golf's etiquette do's and don'ts:

Do	Don't
Be respectful of all players in your group and other groups.	Talk during other players' turns or try to distract them.
Pay attention to the group playing on the hole ahead or behind your own group.	Hit tee shots when the group ahead is still playing that hole.
Leave the putting green and move immediately to the next hole after play of a hole has been completed.	Hang around the green filling out scorecards after everyone has finished putting.
Keep the playing field in good playing shape.	Leave behind divot holes in a fairway or shoe-spike holes on a green after you've finished a hole.

At tournaments, people hold up signs during play that remind people to stay quiet. Players find noise very distracting.

The Pros

The United States has two major professional golf organizations: the Professional Golfers Association (PGA) and the Ladies Professional Golfers Association (LPGA). Founded in 1916, the PGA is the oldest professional association in America. The PGA is the largest sports organization in the world, with more than 27,000 members. People from all over the world come and play on the PGA tour. Professional golfers travel with the tour to many golf courses and play tournaments almost every weekend during the golf season.

The LPGA was formed in 1950 to support women in the sport of professional golf. Before the 1950s, most golf competitions were for men only. Like the PGA, the LPGA organizes competitions for female professional golfers, which is known as the LPGA tour. Female professionals can belong to both the PGA and the LPGA.

Besides the professionals, many amateur golfers enjoy playing the game. The United States Golf Association (USGA) oversees all amateur golf events. The American Junior Golf Association organizes events for young golfers.

Dottie Pepper celebrates a victory on the LPGA tour.

The Majors

Each year, professional golfers compete in many tournaments. They all have one goal: to win a major title. The British Open, U.S. Open, U.S. PGA Championship, and the Masters are the four major professional championships held each year. The four majors are known as the grand slam. Most golfers work their entire lives and never win a major title. In fact, only five players have won all of the majors during their careers! A player who wins all four majors is known as having won a "career grand slam." No one has ever won a professional grand slam in a single season.

David Duval of the U.S. celebrates and kisses his trophy after winning the 2001 British Open Championship.

Around the World

Imagine playing golf in the desert of Saudi Arabia! The sport of golf is known for its beautiful courses and *scenic* locations. *Architects* design the layout of each course. Each architect tries to make his or her course the most challenging and beautiful in the world.

Several courses are famous and have become legends in the sport. Amateur and professional golfers alike dream about stepping on the green and playing a round of golf at these legendary courses.

Golfers play the seventh hole at Pebble Beach. The golf course borders the Pacific Ocean, and most of the holes have amazing views of the water.

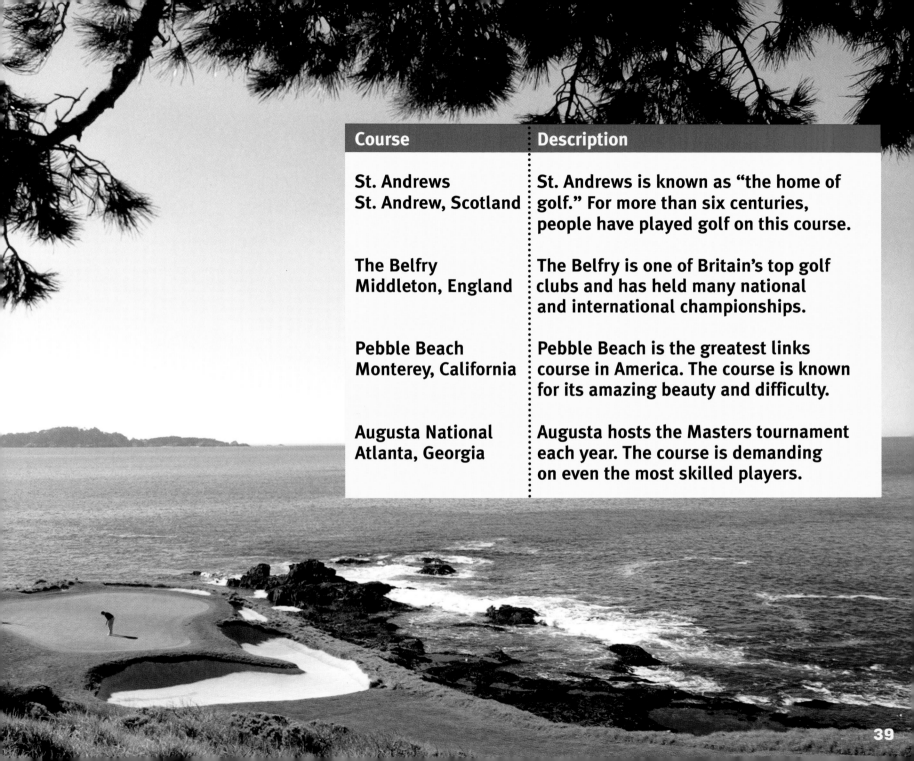

Course	Description
St. Andrews St. Andrew, Scotland	St. Andrews is known as "the home of golf." For more than six centuries, people have played golf on this course.
The Belfry Middleton, England	The Belfry is one of Britain's top golf clubs and has held many national and international championships.
Pebble Beach Monterey, California	Pebble Beach is the greatest links course in America. The course is known for its amazing beauty and difficulty.
Augusta National Atlanta, Georgia	Augusta hosts the Masters tournament each year. The course is demanding on even the most skilled players.

Legends

Thousands of players have contributed to golf's long, rich history. Babe Didrikson Zaharias and Tiger Woods are two of the game's best.

Babe Didrikson Zaharias

Mildred (Babe) Didrikson Zaharias is perhaps the greatest all-around athlete of all time. She was born on June 26, 1914, in Port Arthur, Texas. Mildred earned the nickname "Babe" after she hit five home runs in a single baseball game. In 1932, she earned three medals at the Summer Olympic Games in the javelin and long jump. Zaharias took up golf in 1935. During her golf career, she won 55 professional and amateur events, including ten major titles. In 1949, she helped found the LPGA. In 1950, the AP chose her as the "Athlete of the Half Century." She died in 1956 at the age of 42.

Tiger Woods

Eldrick (Tiger) Woods may be the greatest golfer of all time. He accomplished more by the age of 27 than most golfers do in a lifetime. He was born on December 30, 1975, in Cypress, California. Since age two, Tiger has been perfecting his golf game. He had an impressive amateur career before he turned professional in 1996. Since 1996, he has won 47 tournaments, including eight major championship titles. He was the first major championship winner of African or Asian heritage. In 2000, Tiger Woods became the fifth golfer ever to achieve a career grand slam. Because of his dominance and skill, people expect him to continue his amazing achievements in the years to come.

What Happened When?

1350   **1500**   **1600**   **1700**   **1800**   **1900**

1353 The first recorded reference to chole, the game that evolved into golf.

1421 Hugh Kennedy, Robert Stewart, and John Smale introduce the game of golf to Scotland.

SCOTLAND

1502 King James IV makes the first recorded purchase of golf equipment. He bought a set of clubs from a bow-maker.

1552 Golfers play at St. Andrews for the first time.

1567 Mary, Queen of Scots, becomes the first known female golfer.

Mary, Queen of Scots

1682 Players from Scotland and England compete in the first international golf match.

1754 The St. Andrews Golfers publish the first *Rules of Golf*.

1857 H.B. Farnie publishes *The Golfer's Manual*. It is the first book on golf instruction.

1861 Golfers compete in the first British Open.

1867 The Ladies' Golf Club at St. Andrews is founded, which is the first golf club for women.

1892 Players compete in the Amateur Golf Championship of India and the East—the first international championship event.

1894 The United States Golf Association (USGA) is founded.

1895 Players compete in the first U.S. Open.

1905 William Taylor patents the first dimple-pattern golf ball.

1913 France and the U.S. compete in the first international professional golf match.

1916 The Professional Golfers Association (PGA) of America is founded by 35 charter members.

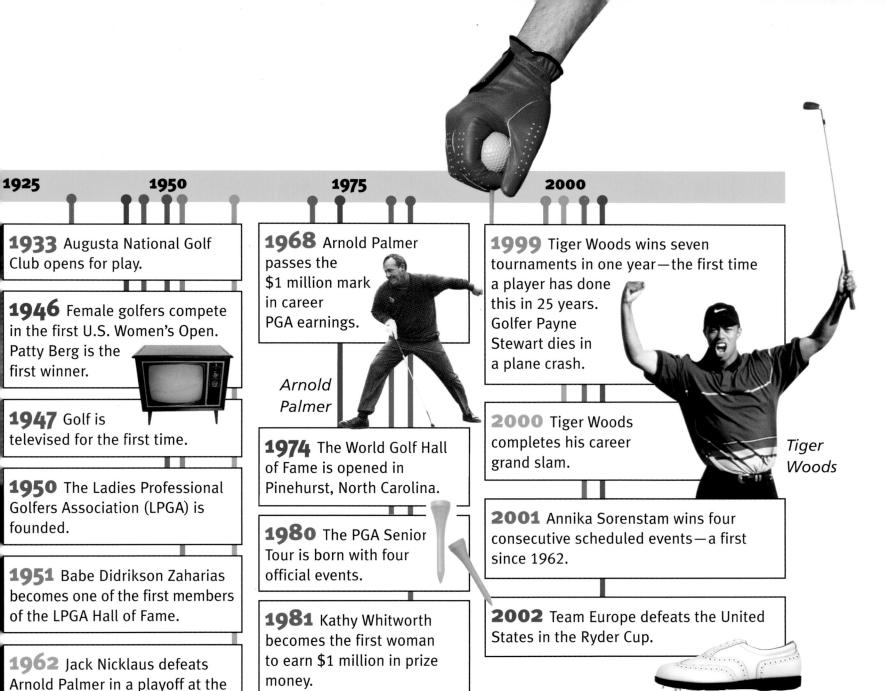

1925	1950	1975	2000

1933 Augusta National Golf Club opens for play.

1946 Female golfers compete in the first U.S. Women's Open. Patty Berg is the first winner.

1947 Golf is televised for the first time.

1950 The Ladies Professional Golfers Association (LPGA) is founded.

1951 Babe Didrikson Zaharias becomes one of the first members of the LPGA Hall of Fame.

1962 Jack Nicklaus defeats Arnold Palmer in a playoff at the U.S. Open.

1968 Arnold Palmer passes the $1 million mark in career PGA earnings.

Arnold Palmer

1974 The World Golf Hall of Fame is opened in Pinehurst, North Carolina.

1980 The PGA Senior Tour is born with four official events.

1981 Kathy Whitworth becomes the first woman to earn $1 million in prize money.

1999 Tiger Woods wins seven tournaments in one year—the first time a player has done this in 25 years. Golfer Payne Stewart dies in a plane crash.

2000 Tiger Woods completes his career grand slam.

Tiger Woods

2001 Annika Sorenstam wins four consecutive scheduled events—a first since 1962.

2002 Team Europe defeats the United States in the Ryder Cup.

Great Golf Facts

A course with all par-three holes is called an executive course.

Golfers used to wear knickers when they played the game! Knickers are a special type of pant that come just below the knee.

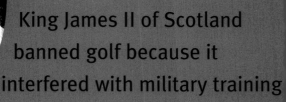

The "dance floor" is another name for the putting green. Some golfers do a little jig, or dance, after they sink a difficult putt. This is where the nickname comes from.

King James II of Scotland banned golf because it interfered with military training

What is a mulligan? In a friendly game of golf, players allow each other to repeat a bad shot without counting penalty strokes—called a "mulligan."

Mary, Queen of Scots, invented the caddie. She used military cadets to carry her clubs. Over time "cadet" became shortened to "caddie."

When a golfer hits a putt that is well short of the hole, they say, "Nice putt, Alice." No one knows who Alice was, but it was believed that she never hit the ball hard enough into the hole. Both males and females make this comment to each other.

A ball buried in a pocket of sand in a bunker is called a fried egg! The ball looks like an egg in a frying pan, which is where the term comes from.

Golf Words to Know

caddie: a person who carries the clubs during a round of golf; also gives players advice and keeps track of their score

divot: a chunk of grass and dirt chopped out of the ground during a swing; also a hole made by a golfer's shoes, or cleats

drive: a shot made from the teeing area except on par-three holes

fairway: the surface that runs from the tee to the green

hazard: an area of sand or water where the player cannot ground the club

hole out: to complete play on a hole

iron: a club with a flat, bladelike head; usually used for longer shots

lie: the position of the ball on the ground

links course: a course located along the sea

long irons: the number one-, two-, three-, and four-iron clubs

out-of-bounds: when the ball is outside the boundary of the golf course

pairing: a group of two players

par: the number of strokes an expert golfer would use to finish playing a hole

putt: a short shot used on the green to move the ball into the hole

putter: a straight-faced club used on the green

rough: the area on a golf course through the green that has high grass or trees but is still playable

round: playing nine or 18 holes of golf

short game: shots played on and around the green

stroke: a swing of the club at the ball

teeing area: the area at the beginning of a hole where a player can tee the ball and start

unplayable lie: when the ball lands in an unplayable position on the course

wedge: a club used for accurate shots during the last 100 yards of playing a hole; the difference among wedges is the amount of clubhead loft

wood: a club with a fat, rounded head on the side behind the face that strikes the ball; usually used for tee-shots or drives

Metric Conversion
1 yard = .9144 meters

Other Words to Know

Here are definitions for some of the words used in this book:

accurately: free from mistakes or errors

arc: something shaped like a curve or arch

architect: a person who designs things

courteous: being considerate to other people

disqualified: eliminated from the game

maximum: the greatest amount allowed

obstacle: something that stands in the way of a person or thing

penalized: being punished for breaking the rules

professional: a person paid to do a job or play a game

scenic: having beautiful views

sphere: a round, solid object

unique: the only one of its kind

Where To Learn More

AT THE LIBRARY

Gordon, John. *The Kids Book of Golf.* Toronto: Kids Can Press, Limited, 2001.

Simmons, Richard. *Superguides: Golf.* New York: DK Publishing, Inc., 2001.

ON THE ROAD

World Golf Hall of Fame
1 World Golf Place
St. Augustine, FL 32092
904/940-4000
http://www.wwgv.com/hof/hof.html

USGA Golf House and Museum
Liberty Corner Road (Rt 512)
Far Hills, NJ 07931
908/234-2300
http://www.usga.org/golfhouse

ON THE WEB

For more information on golf, use FactHound to track down Web sites related to this book.

1. Go to www.facthound.com
2. Type in this book ID: 0756504864
3. Click on the *FETCH IT* button.

Your trusty FactHound will fetch the best Web sites for you!

INDEX

ABOUT THE AUTHOR

Sandra Will graduated magna cum laude from Barnard College, Columbia University, with a B.A. degree in English Literature. Sandra's passion for sports stems from her childhood. When she is not watching a game, she enjoys reading books, visiting museums, and playing with her dog, Maggie. Originally from Chehalis, Washington, Sandra lives in New York City.